Testimonials

"If you are looking for a high energy individual that will put you on the road to success then Cory Mosley is your man. I have always admired Cory's passion and straight talk and he has grown to become not only a great person to do business with but also a friend."
-Todd Smith, Founder & CEO, 360 Converge

"Cory knows the consulting business inside and out. Combine that knowledge with his integrity, engaging training techniques, marketing savvy, and proven sales strategies, and you have one business powerhouse. Even if you're not looking for a coach or consultant today, you owe it to yourself to have a conversation with Cory Mosley. Put him in your Rolodex today, your business tomorrow, and you'll put him top of your "Thank You" list for years to come."
-Mike Parson, Founder & CEO, Laser Stream Video

"Cory is one of the finest consultants that I know. He is a true asset to any company that needs professional consulting, coaching, or sales training." **-Jack Behar, Founder & CEO, InteractiveTel**

"Cory is a leader and has the drive and knowledge to maintain that position. He is a thoughtful, accountable advisor and consultant in a time when businesses are significantly lacking in those traits. When someone puts the focus into their profession as Cory does, everyone wins. Cory has my recommendation for any organization looking to improve." **-Gary May, Founder & CEO, IM@CS**

"Besides Cory's fabulous personality, he demonstrates professionalism and brings to the table devotion and motivation on any project. He is up front and a no-nonsense professional in every sense of the word." **-Ann Shallcross, President, FB Digital**

Entrepreneurship Confidential

Strategies & Real Talk for First-Time Entrepreneurs

Cory Mosley

For Xiomara, my biggest fan, confidant, and cheerleader

Table of Contents

Introduction

Legendary motivational speaker Les Brown is noted as saying "some people just aren't mentally fit to work for other people", and boy has that statement spoken to me my entire life. Like most, I have "formally" worked for other people and I use the term "formally" to speak specifically to the traditional employee/employer dynamic. Let me clear to say that even as an entrepreneur I still work for people every day, they just happened to be my clients and customers.

During each job that I held I always knew in the back of my mind, it was just a pit stop and not a destination. I suspect that you may be getting ready to embark on your journey into entrepreneurship because you have had the same feeling.

This book is a collection of articles and blogs that I have written to tackle some of the conventional and lesser talked about topics that entrepreneurs need to know about. I've also added motivational messages that I believe entrepreneurs need to hear.

I've had the opportunity to work with all types of businesses including several fortune 500 companies, but nothing is more rewarding than being able to contribute to the growth of an individual person, especially those bitten by the entrepreneurship bug.

Please take this information to heart, let it add value to your journey, and always make sure you do the work.

To your success,
Cory

- Part 1 -
MATTERS OF THE MIND

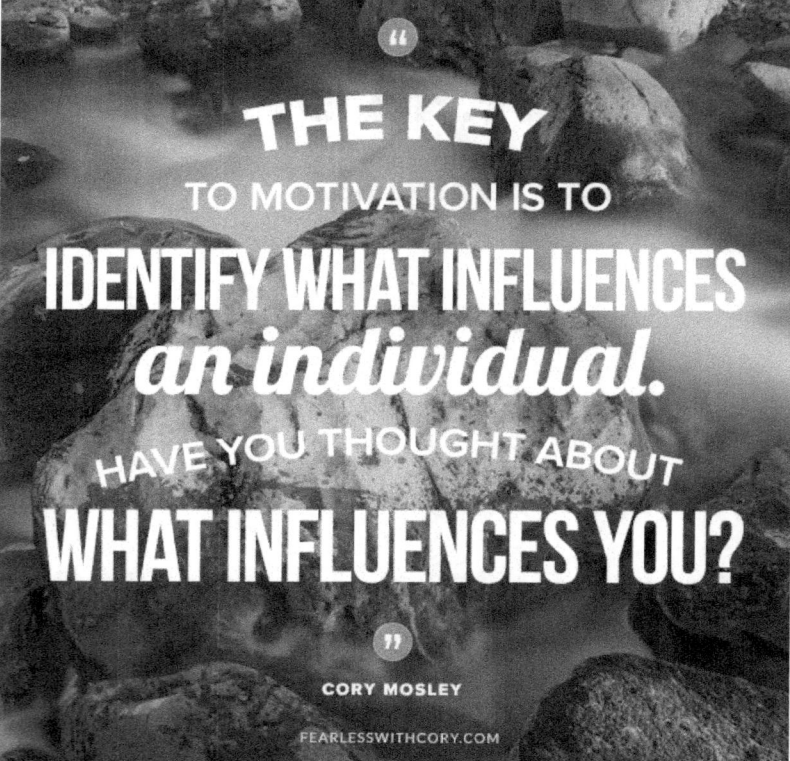

Right Job for You: Side Gig Cash or Full-Time Commitment?

When it comes to *side hustles, part-time work, and the gig economy*, it turns out a lot of people do it for a variety of reasons[1]:

- The **side hustle** includes any money-making venture as short as answering online surveys or management projects lasting a year or more. The Bureau of Labor Statistics refers to these workers as contingent workers; those whose have no contract for long-term employment.

- Between two and four percent of all workers fall into the bureau's definition of contingent workers.

- The number of contingent workers and independent contractors in the workforce is growing in all business sectors, with maintenance/repair, personal care, and civic organizations gaining the most.

- The BLS Occupational Outlook Handbook lists single-task jobs as those most likely to attract contingent and contractor workers, including construction, transportation, print and digital news media, musicians, fine artists, computer programmers, coders, and software developers.

WHY START A SIDE HUSTLE (AND KEEP IT THERE):

Your Time Is Your Own:

You decide what jobs to accept and reject. Scheduling flexibility is critical for many workers caring for young children or elderly parents without assistance from daycare facilities or home health care.

Your Time Is Your Money:

You set your fees and decide what your work is worth. How competitive you are depends on a number of factors, including your hourly or per-job rate.

No Two Days Are Alike:

If a day of diverse work appeals to you, the side hustle provides that variety.

You Work Your Passion:

A side job pays more than money; it feeds a need to do what you love. Many gig workers use their full-time jobs to pay bills and feed families, while the side job finances future entrepreneurial endeavors.

You Stay Really Busy:

Working 50, 60 or more hours a week is possible in the side job/regular job scenario. That's exhausting for many people, but some find it exhilarating; work is not just a goal for them, but their daily fix of fuel and fire.

You Experiment Without Significant Investment:

Work the part-time job from your home office or a shared space, without the big startup costs necessary for a full-time commitment.

You Keep Your Full-Time Job's Benefits:

Maintain your full-time job, and keep your health insurance, investment, and other employee benefits.

WHY TURN THE SIDE HUSTLE INTO A FULL-TIME JOB:

Full-Time Means Access To Benefits:

Going full-time is a chance to incorporate the business and become a legally registered entity in your state. This creates an opportunity to gain tax benefits, raise capital, protect yourself from personal liability and present yourself in the most professional light possible.

Less Money Coming In:

The side job is a time thief, and more time spent does not always translate to more money. Unhappy clients, unforeseen delays, technical glitches and excessive travel cost money. Full-time includes full attention to all the details.

Side Hustles Can Be So Unreliable:

You may have 10 clients a month, or one. You deliver three months' work to a client and they disappear without paying. A few hours a week or month isn't enough time to keep up with the demands.

It Shows Clients Your Commitment And Discipline:

A client with a year-long project approaches you; the part-time you cannot handle the timeline; the full-time you say, "Yes and thank you; I want this project and it will be done to all your specifications."

Consistent Scheduling:

Full-time commitment means simpler, easier scheduling, instead of working extra jobs around available hours.

HOW DO YOU DECIDE WHAT WORKS FOR YOU?

Ask Yourself

"What do I want to be when I grow up?: Do you see yourself working the job-and-a-half for life, fervently pursuing your passion or maintaining the safe but monotonous nine-to-five until retirement?

Look At Your Budget Needs:

Do you have enough saved for six to 12 months' worth of bills in order to declare your dream ready for the full-time responsibility?

Think Long Term:

Retirement and future medical expenses loom large in your

budget as you get older. Passion pays when you work hard and smart, but pay yourself first: do you have sufficient discipline to save most of what you make for the future and to invest back into the business.

Are You Risk Averse Or Risk Seeking?

Be honest: do you enjoy taking chances, daring failure while courting success and not knowing what next week, next month or next year looks like? Or are you the proverbial smooth sailing type who prefers calm water to waves and predictable weather to possible storms?

Ask Someone Who's Been There:

Seek a mentor in the business you're starting or a professional coach who listens asks the hard questions provides the answers you don't always want to hear and offers the guidance learned from hard work, hustle, successes and even some failures. No matter how you start, setbacks happen even as you move forward. Read the consultant's work, listen to their talks and watch their videos to learn new insights and avoid problems.

Raise the bar
and your standards.

Break from the
comfort zone
that has become
your daily routine

and push yourself into
Unchartered Territory.

Breaking Free From the 6 Fears Entrepreneurs Face

Entrepreneurs launch their dreams thinking they are boarding a cruise ship. Then we realize we actually boarded a battleship. The good news is that this is what makes entrepreneurs who they are. We thrive on the challenge.

There are two ways you can set out and face the battles ahead. You can jump then find out what struggles await you as you go. When they arise, you figure it out and fight your way through. Or you can brace yourself for the impact.

You can find out what battles lie ahead and get yourself ready. Put a plan in place. And decide beforehand how you're going to handle the tension. To do it that way, you need to know what the battles are. That's why we're going to look at the 6 major fears entrepreneurs face and ultimately must overcome to be successful. Exploring them together today will help us prepare for what to do before they occur. So, let's jump in.

1. FINANCIAL PRESSURES

If you've ever had to decide on whether to get your baby formula or diapers you know what it feels like to be an entrepreneur. Sometimes, we have to make a decision. Do we buy inventory or do we use the money to advertise? Both are essential, but we don't have the funds for both. This puts a lot of pressure on you to make wise financial decisions. To delegate resources strategically. And to convince everyone else around you why the one purchase is better than the other.

2. REJECTION

It's tough to have VC reps tell you they see no benefit in investing in your startup. Cold emails get rejection replies if they even generate a reply at all. And you have to stay convinced that what you are doing is good for your market. That they need what you have even when they keep telling you that you have nothing.

3. LONELINESS

This is both physical and mental. In some cases, you are alone. Literally. You are the creative team. The boss. The finance department. The sales rep. Everything. It is you, yourself, and nobody else. But even if you have some people to help, you will still fight this battle. It is lonely at the top. People won't understand your goals or ideas. And no one else will care about your organization as much as you do. Regardless of how much buy-in you have, and even if they're amazing employees, they still will not be as passionate as you are. And that can be a very lonely feeling.

4. CRITICISM

You will hear any and every reason as to why you won't succeed. Your boss will tell you you're crazy for quitting your job to start a dream. And your family may tell you the same. Even your close friends will laugh and "encourage" you to stop and think about what you're doing. You have to be sold on your idea before you tell anyone about it. Because once you let everyone know what you want to do, they will be sure to let you know why you can't.

5. INADEQUACY

As an entrepreneur, you have to be confident. And this has to bleed out of you. You have to know what you're doing and how to do it. And people around you need to sense that competency. You won't be able to succeed otherwise. But at the end of the day, when it's just you, you will sense that you aren't as confident as you'd like. You will feel that you are not resourceful enough to come up with the solutions to all the problems that arise. But you have to push forward anyway. It's not that you are inadequate. It's that the road of entrepreneurship will try to convince you that you are. And it will do so with such persuasiveness that it will make you feel like you are. And you will have to push forward in spite of how you feel. When you do, your feelings will follow. Eventually, you will see that you do have what it takes. But that certainty comes after the battle, not before it. The basic road is something like this. First: I think I can do this. Second: There is no way I can do this. Third: Ok, I see I can do this. Although that breakdown looks simple on screen, it's an accurate representation of the battle you will face. And the transition from the second phase to the third phase is much easier to read than to live. But the entrepreneurs who live it are the ones you hear about. The ones who don't are the ones you never know of. It's up to you to decide which type of entrepreneur you are going to be.

6. DISCOURAGEMENT

The reason discouragement is last on the list is because it's not a battle in and of itself. It is the result of the other 6 battles combined. When you have to decide between paying employees or buying inventory while constantly being rejected, feeling alone, hearing the criticism, and sensing your own inadequacy, the result is an overwhelming sense of discouragement. As an entrepreneur, you've got to battle through this. You have to keep the dream alive and push through your pain. You cannot allow the other 6 battles to overwhelm you into this battle of discouragement. You will feel this, but you don't have to get stuck here. The key is to learn how to encourage yourself and push beyond the setbacks. When you do, the feelings of discouragement will change. You will sense hope in spite of all the difficulty.

IN MOST CASES, ALL 6 OF THESE BATTLES WILL ARISE.

Knowing what to do beforehand will prepare you to plow through them and to push on towards your dream. Don't be set back. Let each obstacle be a setup. A setup for you to innovate. A setup for you to grow. A setup for you to succeed. Just because you will face a battle doesn't mean you have to shrink back. You can rise to the challenge and thrive to the ultimate accomplishment of your entrepreneurial goal.

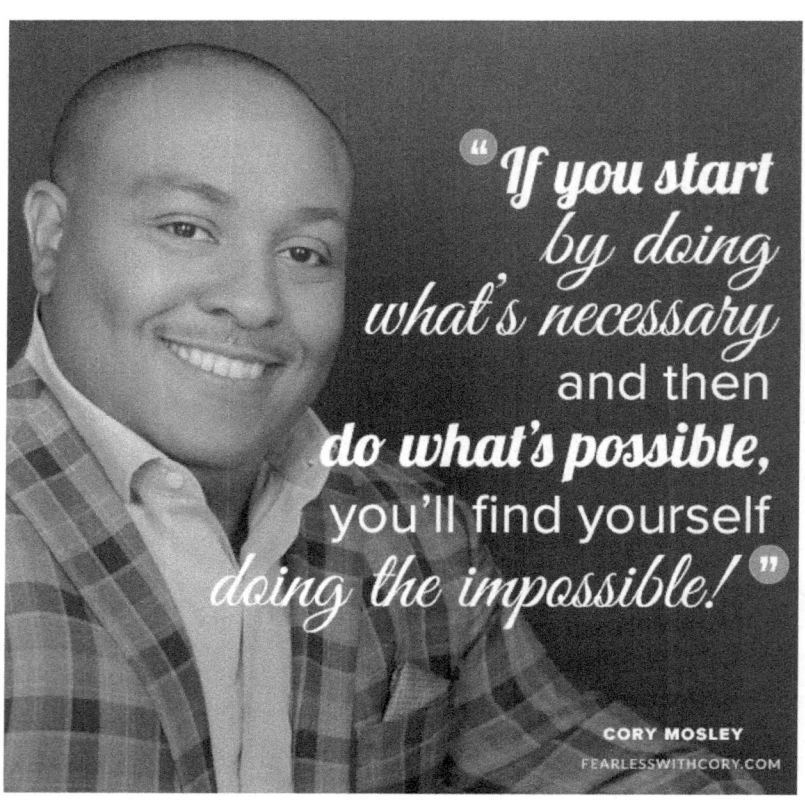

"If you start by doing what's necessary and then do what's possible, you'll find yourself doing the impossible!"

CORY MOSLEY
FEARLESSWITHCORY.COM

Conquering 4 Fears Successful Entrepreneurs Overcome

Did you know that successful entrepreneurs are no less afraid than anyone else?

Just like you or anybody with a dream, entrepreneurs feel the same intensity of stress, anxiety, and fear.

The difference is that we overcome those fears while others stay stuck in them.

If you thought that to be an effective entrepreneur you had to sense no fear you are requiring something that is impossible. As a human being, you will sense fear. The key is not to be without fear. It is to act in spite of the fear you feel.

So what are the **fears that entrepreneurs face?** And more importantly, how do they overcome them?

Let's explore the 4 most common ones and see what successful entrepreneurs do to act in spite of each of them.

1. FEAR OF CRITICISM

Stepping out and trying something new — something that goes against the grain — is difficult.

The actual task itself isn't easy, but when you add to it the fact that friends and family will have their opinion it makes it all the more arduous.

When you leave your 9-5 and hear your coworkers laugh you out the door because your decision to quit and start your own business is "unwise," you will have to bear the pressure.

Sure, it's easy to read this blog and say, "I don't care what people think. I'm an entrepreneur, and I will build my dream." What's not easy is to smile and maintain that position internally when the people you've been friends with for years are standing next to you and are actually saying it. That's when it's tough.

So, what do successful entrepreneurs do?

We bear it. We smile and remain polite. We treat them with courtesy and respect. But we do not allow their words to deter us. In spite of what they say, we pursue our plans and build our ideas into successful enterprises anyways.

2. FEAR OF FAILURE

One of the most paralyzing questions every entrepreneur hears constantly is, "what if this doesn't work?" Not that we hear it from others. In fact, most of the time, the people around us encourage us to pursue our dreams (for the most part.)

It's not what we hear other say. It's what we hear ourselves say to ourselves.

What if this doesn't work? What if I fail? What if I mess up?

It has been said that we should not answer a question with a question. But that does not apply here. The way successful entrepreneurs deal with this particular fear is by asking a different question.

When the question arises, "What if this fails?" successful entrepreneurs ask instead, "What if this works?"

"What if this works?" is the best response to "What if this fails?"

By asking this question instead, we refocus our thoughts and channel them in the exact opposite direction. Instead of focusing on all the bad that can result if we fail, we focus on all the good that will happen when we do.

And that makes all the difference.

3. FEAR OF SUCCESS

This point may strike you as odd at first, but it's actually a deep-rooted fear that most entrepreneurs are unaware of but almost all of us have to face.

The fear of success is closely linked to a fear of what people think about us. Before you write this one off, consider if you've ever thought any of the following ideas.

What will my neighbors think if I get rich?

My uncle will assume I think I'm better than him if I become successful in business.

My friends may want a handout when my idea goes big.

How will people perceive me when I drive up in a new car?

The fear of success is a very real fear that actually keeps entrepreneurs stuck. It makes some of them sabotage their own success through procrastination, intentional errors, rude communications, etc.

All in an attempt to prevent one from actually achieving the success that will ultimately alter the way everyone in the entrepreneur's life will perceive him moving forward.

4. FEAR OF WORK SCHEDULES

Many people have two extreme misconceptions about entrepreneurs. Some people think we wake up at 10:30 am and drink coffee in our pajamas while we work for an hour then clock out for the rest of the day by noon. Others assume we work from 6 am to midnight 7 days a week.

The truth is that both extremes occur at times but, for the most part, we live somewhere in the middle. We have a balanced work life as does the majority of the working class.

The problem is that some entrepreneurs fear that they have to fit one of those two extremes. Either they assume that working more than an hour a day is not what "modern-entrepreneurs" do. So, they work very little and ultimately achieve very small results. This, in turn, frustrates them.

The other group of entrepreneurs fall prey to the idea that working hard, all the time, is the way to succeed. They try to live up to this ideal and quickly burn out. The result of this extreme is the same as the first one — they end up with very small results.

Not understanding the balance of work schedules in the lives of real entrepreneurs, many new entrepreneurs deal with the fear of what their work schedule will look like.

To combat this, successful entrepreneurs learn what works for them and find a flow that fits.

There is no one-size fits all approach.

Consider, for example, Bill Gates and Warren Buffet. These two men usually hold the first and second spots for the richest men in the world although that does fluctuate a little. Ultimately though, both men are entrepreneurs and both are extremely successful.

Bill Gates schedules his days by the minute. Everything is preassigned and put on his calendar. Warren Buffet, on the other hand, holds few to no meetings and just goes with the flow allowing his days to unfold as they do.

Neither is right or wrong. But each one found what fits them.

When it comes to finding the best schedule, every entrepreneur overcomes this fear by finding what works for their own style, gifting, and personality.

Usually, however, it is neither a one hour a day or 75 hours a week approach that produces success.

It is normally something in the middle — a balanced overall approach with an occasional tip to one side or the other based on the season of life the entrepreneur is in at any given point in time.

All in all, entrepreneurs face fears the same way everyone else does. We fear criticism, failure, success, and scheduling as does any other human being with thoughts and feelings.

The difference is that we face those fears head-on, and we find ways to work around them successfully.

ACCEPT
YOUR GREATNESS

EVEN IF

IT'S UNDER
CONSTRUCTION.

CORY MOSLEY
FEARLESSWITHCORY.COM

Impostor Syndrome – The Aspiring Entrepreneur's Silent Success Killer

As an **aspiring entrepreneur**, you have probably faced moments of doubt. You begin to wonder if you are really good enough, if you can really achieve your goals, and if you will ever find real success in your career. While these feelings may be discouraging, the good news is that as a first-time entrepreneur, you are not alone. Many others in your position are also dealing with that has been termed "Impostor Syndrome."

Impostor syndrome encompasses a wide range of feelings. It includes worrying that you aren't smart enough, talented enough, or good enough to achieve your dream. As an aspiring entrepreneur, you might fear that others will find out that you really aren't as smart or as good at your job as they assumed. Sometimes, people begin to think that it was luck, not skill, that helped them to achieve success. While some people allow Impostor Syndrome to discourage them from achieving their dreams, it can also encourage people to work harder, helping them to prove to themselves as well as others that they can achieve their dream.

EVEN THE MOST SUCCESSFUL PEOPLE DEAL WITH IT

When you are dealing with Impostor Syndrome, you may begin to feel like no one else has felt the way you feel. You might start to feel that everyone else is confident and like you are the only one simply pretending to feel confident. Yet, an estimated *70 percent* of people in the United States have faced Impostor Syndrome. Some of the most successful people in the United States can be counted among those who have faced it during their career.[2]

A recent *Entrepreneur* article talked about some people who have admitted to dealing with Impostor Syndrome. For example, Facebook COO Sheryl Sandberg said that during college at Harvard, she felt like she didn't deserve to be there. She said, "There are still days when I wake up feeling like a fraud, not sure I should be where I am." Supreme Court Judge Sonia Sotomayor said she sometimes does not feel like she is completely a part of the world she occupies. She also admits that sometimes she wonders if she measures up to what is expected of her. Others, including successful entrepreneurs, actors, and musicians, have also admitted to feeling a bit like a fraud at times.[3]

THE NEGATIVITY OF IT

Unfortunately, if you allow the negative feelings to take over, Impostor Syndrome can destroy you as a first-time entrepreneur. An Inc. article from last summer talked about how Impostor Syndrome can destroy people's chances of success. People begin sabotaging their own success. Because they doubt themselves, they fail to try their hardest. Sometimes, they think if they stay in the shadows, not standing out too much, others will not realize they are actually a fraud. They may also talk themselves out of doing something they really want to do, convincing themselves that they'll just fail anyway. Unfortunately, this lack of confidence in themselves and their reluctance to take chances may prevent the person from achieving entrepreneurial success.[4]

SEE THE GOOD IN IMPOSTOR SYNDROME

Ultimately, one important key to moving from an aspiring entrepreneur to a successful entrepreneur is to use Impostor Syndrome to your advantage. While it can bring you down, discouraging you, and preventing you from achieving your goals, it can also be a great thing. Realizing that you are not perfect and that you need to work harder to be your best could help you to become your best.

One way to see the good in Impostor Syndrome is to talk about it with others who may be facing the same feelings. While many entrepreneurs are reluctant to admit that they doubt their own abilities, admitting it can help others, who may feel the same way. Impostor Syndrome may also help you to be more careful. While being too cautious on your path to entrepreneurial success is not a good thing, double-checking yourself and thinking through an idea will help you avoid blind confidence. In the end, allowing yourself to fail sometimes and accepting that entrepreneurial success may take time will help you fight Impostor Syndrome. When you are feeling down on yourself, remember to focus on your successes, even if your successes feel small.

Success finds people who focus **not only** on what they know, but on what they can *Actually Do.*

CORY MOSLEY
FEARLESSWITHCORY.COM

How Much Does Passion Pay for First-Time Entrepreneurs?

When you work for an employer and consider striking out alone, there are many thought processes to complete. The biggest one is running the company and then keeping all the profits. This comes in time to some business owners, but you must be willing to give up the economic stability associated with traditional jobs. There is also the fear that your dream of owning a business will meet with skepticism from family and friends, and you don't want to let them down. Finally, there's the notion of getting paid to do what you love but, with business ownership, this passion could quickly become a chore. Suddenly, your passion cuts into your evenings and weekends. You are working for "free" instead of receiving overtime from your employer. In this post, we consider how much passion pays **first-time entrepreneurs** and what happens when passion gets lost.

HOW WILL YOU GET PAID?

As an aspiring entrepreneur, you will seek a profit either by selling goods or services. Some businesses may offer both. For example, you might have an A/C sales and installation business that also performs maintenance and repairs to existing systems. You might make a profit from equipment sales as well as from labor performed on all types of A/C systems. Many entrepreneurs plan to reinvest any profits made back into the company, but they need enough personal savings to cover their household expenses during that time. To determine if you will turn passion into profits, you must estimate how much income you could earn each month after covering the company's overhead costs.

TALK TO OTHER ENTREPRENEURS

The worst thing to do would be to launch a business without a plan. You're too smart for that! However, a plan doesn't always match what actually happens when you are out there in the entrepreneurial trenches. It helps to talk to other entrepreneurs, either through networking events or through online communities (i.e. LinkedIn) and to get small business coaching when needed. Networking means that you ask entrepreneurs with a similar business model how long it took for them to break even (i.e. to recover all of their startup costs) and to begin drawing a salary. Remember, that they are going to give you advice, but they might not share the whole, unvarnished truth. They may sugar-coat how many hours they invested in their company before earning profits or how they had to keep an outside job to cover their family's bills until the business became successful. Entrepreneurs are a tough breed, and they want to maintain the image of a strong duck who always lets the water run down his back.

CONSIDER YOUR PROFESSIONAL WANTS AND NEEDS

While you are still employed in a traditional job, you can also consider the wants and needs you've explored in the current setting and in past jobs. How many hours are you willing to work each week? How many times are you willing to work a 12-hour to 15-hour day or through the entire weekend? Can you miss important events for family and friends because customers must take precedence over them? Will you work through the holidays? Can you stay motivated without receiving regular feedback from a boss? Can you lead a team when success is not guaranteed?

Owning your own company gives you more control over your work and sometimes affords you the opportunity to keep the financial rewards of the services that you've provided. Business ownership is also full of unpredictability, which means that you might need a secondary income to protect your finances and keep a roof over your head. It's possible to phase yourself into first-time entrepreneurship gradually so that you can work towards a profit margin in your company without losing the economic stability of external employment.

TO BE HAPPY, WE MUST NOT BE TOO CONCERNED WITH OTHERS.

— ALBERT CAMUS

Why Entrepreneurs Need More Laughter, not More Humor

As an entrepreneur, you may not always have a lot of opportunities to laugh with someone else. Watching a comedy may help boost your endorphins, but that just doesn't cut it. Come to find out, you need much more than comedy to boost your morale and keep you going on a bleak Monday morning commute from the bed to the office chair down the hall.

WHAT IS LAUGHTER?

Psychology Today has a lot to say about laughter and it is not all it's cracked up to be. In fact, it really has very little to do with humor.[5]

Laughter is a language all of its own. It is not learned like the language(s) we grow up speaking, but it is innate, already programmed in our DNA. And everyone has the laughter gene.

What causes us to laugh? Believe it or not, it is usually not a joke that causes us to burst into laughter, but rather an interaction with another person. This means that social situations produce much more laughter than non-social situations, such as spending Friday night alone with your marketing funnels.

The best part is that the person you're interacting with doesn't even need to say something funny. It may just be an introduction or a simple question about your day. It's not so much what is said as it is who is saying it and the social connection you have with that person.

WHY ENTREPRENEURS NEED TO INTERACT

Team players laugh more than head honchos in the corporate world. Think of the last time you saw a CEO, president, or owner of a big corporation let out a belly laugh, if at all. That doesn't mean they don't laugh, they have just been conditioned not to laugh when they are at work.

Laughter is subconscious and cannot be conjured up at will. It happens spontaneously and is contagious. This is because it is social. It seems, then, that its purpose is to bring people together, despite cultural differences. Laughter doesn't care about these differences. All brains are wired for subconscious, social interactive laughter.

Take a look at the animal world. When chimpanzees are tickled and laugh, it sounds like panting. It is really *"labored breathing"* which is showing another chimp that it is playing.[6] Laughter exists all throughout the animal kingdom, *even in rats.*[7]

When laughter is suppressed, such as with the CEO, it is to convey a social distancing. In other words, don't get too chummy with your employees. But as an entrepreneur, this may be just what you need. We all know laughter benefits the nervous system and lifts up our moods, but mostly, it brings us together.

WHAT IF I'M ALONE?

Being your own boss is ideal, but it doesn't mean you have to go it alone. There are plenty of ways to interact, whether at events, on social media, webinars, or anywhere else on the Internet. If you're really fortunate, you may even have locals to meet up with who understand your entrepreneurial spirit.

We all need to connect somehow. Isolation isn't healthy. Sometimes it's easy to isolate, especially if you haven't showered in a few days while working on that super ad copy or filtering through digital files hour after hour.

If you are alone or feel alone because you don't have adequate support on the home front, then meeting up and connecting with others is crucial. It's not always easy to be your own boss, so laughter is a way of encouraging you to step out and connect with others more if you don't already do this on a regular basis.

It is easier today more than ever to connect with other people, even individuals we just met or don't know very well. As an entrepreneur, you have a unique perspective to offer the world. Your gift is needed on the forefront to teach and share with others. Connecting with like-minded people is critical. That's why masterminds developed among entrepreneurs.

So get out there and laugh more. It will boost your morale and your work will seem much less mundane on a Monday morning.

Make an effort
to seek out
a fresh perspective
and treat your mind
like an umbrella
which, as you know,
works best
when it's open.

CORY MOSLEY
FEARLESSWITHCORY.COM

Managing Depression for First-Time Entrepreneurs

Many first-time entrepreneurs find themselves in a moment of crisis. After weeks or months of long, difficult workdays, unexpected setbacks and delays, things learned the too-hard way, there often comes a moment where you question your goals, your ability, and your decisions. You wonder if you've come too far down the wrong path, with no idea how to turn back. Maybe you just want to go home and crawl into bed and stay there for a few years.

Many people aren't prepared for how emotionally difficult it can be to start your own business and pursue your passion. And although the sense of getting lost and growing depressed is common, it's not often talked about. Here are some ways that first-time entrepreneurs can defeat emotional downturns and stay motivated:

RELY ON YOUR PEERS WHEN MANAGING DEPRESSION.

It's not always appropriate or desirable to share emotions of doubt or misgiving within your business, even with trusted partners and employees; it risks hurting morale and affecting working relationships. Build a network of other entrepreneurs who will listen, give support, and offer solutions. A peer network understands what you are going through and will be there for you during low moments.

TAKE CARE OF YOURSELF.

This seems easier said than done when feeling the weight and responsibility for the success of your business, but forcing yourself to make time for self-care pays off for you and for your venture. Spend time in nature, do some heart-healthy low-impact exercise, get good sleep, and spend quality time with friends and family. Focusing on relaxing, enjoyable, non-work-related activities not only helps recharge your batteries but can inspire renewed creativity and better solutions at work.

CHALLENGE NEGATIVE THOUGHTS.

Many of our most insidious negative thoughts are automatic, and won't stand up to rational examination. If you find yourself focusing too much on negative thoughts and events, take the time to make a list every day of things that are working and going well. If you find yourself making negative assumptions with no evidence, remind yourself that jumping to negative conclusions is neither helpful nor reasonable. And try not to generalize one setback or failure into widespread negative thinking about your business or yourself.

DIG INTO YOUR PASSION.

Unfortunately, it often happens that a person starts a business because they really want to do the thing they are passionate about, but then find themselves spending the majority of the time on the business itself. While systems, payroll, accounting, development, marketing, infrastructure, recruiting, and management are all tasks that entrepreneurs have to do in order to be successful, remember to make time to do the original work that inspired and excited you, to begin with. Touching base with your passion keeps you grounded and motivated, and makes you a better leader and representative for your business.

The most difficult aspect of depression is that it undermines your ability to do the very things that would help ease depression. It can be pernicious over time. Once depression sets in, it becomes much harder to reach out and form new friendships, get motivated to exercise or be inspired by your passion. That's all the more reason to practice these skills now and make a habit of them so that you have the tools, resources, and resilience necessary to combat emotional setbacks when they come.

The truth is that every first-time entrepreneur faces a task that is difficult and demanding, financially, socially, physically, and emotionally. But it's a task worth doing, in order to share your unique abilities, perspectives, and solutions with the world. Managing depression during this time is very important. Making the time to keep yourself balanced, focused, and healthy, inside and out, benefits you, your business, and the world that waits for you.

– Part 2 –

MATTERS OF THE MIND CONTINUED

Those who **take action** *are More Effective* because they try harder, keep things in *Motion,* accomplish more *in Less Time* and are willing to **take a shot.**

CORY MOSLEY
FEARLESSWITHCORY.COM

The Connection Between Perseverance and Mental Toughness

On the path to success, you are going to run into a few roadblocks. The key is not so much a matter of avoiding these roadblocks as it is continuing despite these roadblocks. One of the keys to persevering despite setback is to develop **mental toughness**. If you are looking to develop mental toughness, there are several things you should do.

MAKE IT A DECISION

In an *Inc. article* from last winter, extreme athletes and special forces soldiers were asked about mental toughness. One suggestion was that you have to make the decision to be mentally tough. This means pushing past the things you think are difficult or that you don't want to do. Prove to yourself that you can do hard things. At times, this might mean passing on that night out with friends so you can get a difficult but important project completed on time. It might also mean not buying something you really want so that money can be invested in your company instead.[8]

In the beginning, it might be difficult to resist the things you want now in favor of the things that will really matter later. As you make the decision to build mental toughness, though, it will become easier and easier to resist those diversions that were once enticing.

SMALL STEPS

Of course, mental toughness is not going to come all at once. When you look at the big picture of what you want to accomplish, it can feel overwhelming and impossible. *Amelia Boone*, an extreme athlete who is a three-time World's Toughest Mudder Champion and a Spartan Race World Champion, said:[9]

> *I find that if you start looking at the overall picture, if you start to see how much further you have to go, that's when you mentally want to check out, and that's when you mentally quit, and so for me, breaking it down into smaller goals helps me through that process.*

One of the keys to achieving a big goal is to break it into smaller parts. If your goal is to build a multi-million-dollar company, it might be discouraging if your company barely breaks even the first quarter. While building a highly successful company is a great goal, start out with something smaller. Maybe this month you are going to try to make three quality business connections. Perhaps, your big goal for the month is to get your website up and running or to have a certain number of visitors on your site. As you achieve these smaller goals, you are building toward your bigger goal while also gaining more confidence in yourself and your ideas.

AVOIDING LIMITING YOURSELF

Often, it becomes easy to set limits for ourselves. We may feel like we can reach a specific goal, but that if we are required to work even a little harder, we won't be able to do it. The problem is that success is often somewhere just beyond what we perceive as our limit. In an *Entrepreneur* article from this summer, one lady talked about how climbing Mount Kilimanjaro taught her that she could keep going even when she felt like she could go no further. When you feel like you have reached your limit, push just a little harder. You might be surprised what you can achieve.

BELIEVE IN YOURSELF

Perhaps one of the most important things you can do to achieve your dreams is to believe in yourself. There will likely be people who will try to tell you that what you want to achieve is impossible or that you aren't smart enough, dedicated enough, good enough, or otherwise enough to achieve your dream. At times, the voice saying this might be the voice in your head. The key to achieving your goal is to not allow that voice, no matter how loud or strong, to discourage you. Keeping believing in yourself.[10]

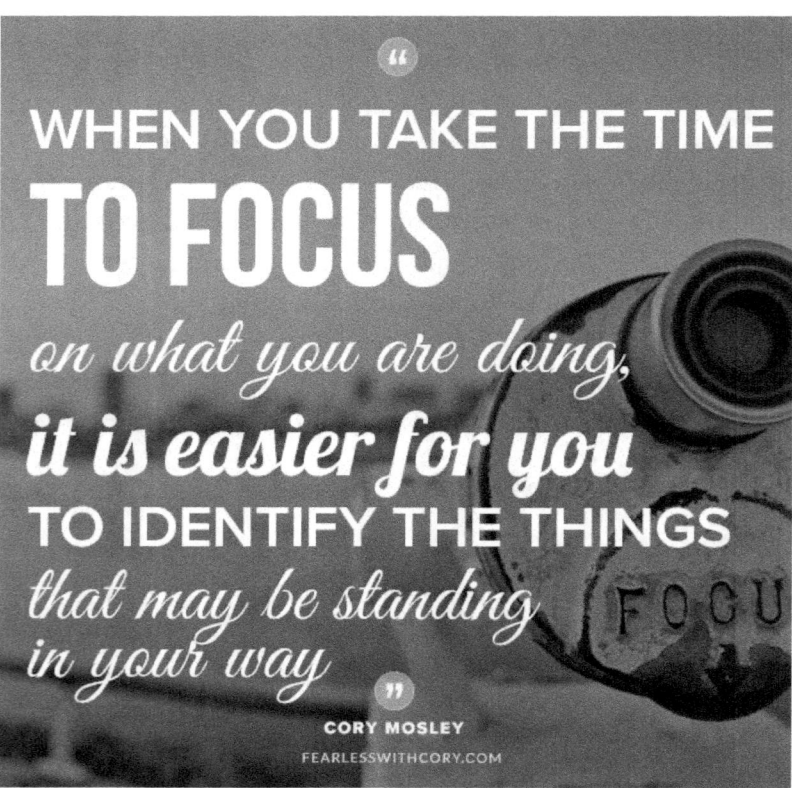

"

WHEN YOU TAKE THE TIME
TO FOCUS
on what you are doing,
it is easier for you
TO IDENTIFY THE THINGS
that may be standing
in your way

"

CORY MOSLEY
FEARLESSWITHCORY.COM

The 4 C's to Help you Find Your Focus

Few things give rise to the idea that you can do a job better, faster and make more money on your own than a bad day at the corporate office. We're talking about a three-strikes-you're-out, should-have-stayed-in-bed kind of bad day. Sometimes the day never gets on track, or one delayed project, missed meeting or ugly email derails everything. The key to managing the messes and repairing the damage is focus: the ability to look through, above and around the noise and concentrate on the required task. **Focus** requires creativity, concentration, confidence and cooperation, and how much you accomplish depends on how you develop and use these skills.

CREATIVITY

Make a to-do list every day: The list confirms your day's activities, provides purpose, organization, and structure and establishes daily, weekly and monthly rituals, reminding your brain regularly of those tasks needing your attention.

Allocate your time around your tasks, not the other way around: Be deliberate in your time management skills. A slapdash list of chores and eight hours to do them translates to all of them squeezed into the last two hours. Instead, each job receives a specified amount of time for completion, with some flexibility allowed.

Incorporate fun time: Mental downtime is necessary for brain training. When you train your body, your muscles require rest time to heal injury, soreness and rebuild tissue. It's the same for your brain. Keep fun brain training games (such as crossword puzzles, word search games) close by or on your *phone or tablet*, and enjoy them as a break and brain builder.[11]

Exercise is essential: Regular workouts lower weight, blood pressure, blood sugar and stress levels, and also release a *chemical* in the brain aiding in memory function and mental sharpness. Exercising once or twice a week is not enough to help; you need to break a moderate sweat five times a week to gain this advantage.[12]

CONCENTRATION

Know where you do your best work: Some people thrive in chaos, while others require quiet. Provide yourself with the environment that works for you.

Keep multitasking to a minimum: It's rewarding to do many things at once, thinking we get a lot accomplished. But it's also a distraction from critical tasks when our attention fluctuates from one activity to another.

What happens at work stays at work: Keep work and personal life separate. We're tempted to bring work home and proudly lay claim to working too hard. But spreading work over so many hours invites distraction, exhaustion and decreases concentration.

Practice the art of the focused mind: Treat your brain like the rest of your muscles, and train it every day by doing one task for five minutes, then increasing the time every day.

CONFIDENCE

Believe you can do at least one difficult thing daily: Have a tough conversation with a loved one, take care of your will, pay off an old credit card debt or reconnect with a former friend or colleague you dislike. These are uncomfortable situations that breed confidence with successful contact and conclusion.

Know where you are going: Have a written six month, one year and five-year plan of action. Dreaming is the first part of your decision process; definitive results require decisive steps.

Adopt a mantra and repeat it every day: Post it on a wall or the bathroom mirror. Listen to your favorite motivational speaker's most inspiring speech. Remind yourself first thing in the morning and last thing at night: I have a goal. I will only find it if I keep looking and moving forward.

Look and dress the part before you get the part: In business, you always dress for the job you want, not the job you have. Potential clients want to meet and give business to someone who is dressed and groomed properly.

COOPERATION

Have trusted friends, teachers, and mentors: It's not weak or wrong to ask questions; it's foolish thinking you can truly enter the entrepreneur's world alone. Join business clubs, attend chamber of commerce meetings, sign up for conventions and enroll in classes.

Be honest with friends and family: Tell them about your decision to become a business, instead of working for one. Some will support you, others will walk away. Avoid judgments and arguments, accept their opinions and show gratitude to those who promise to stand with you.

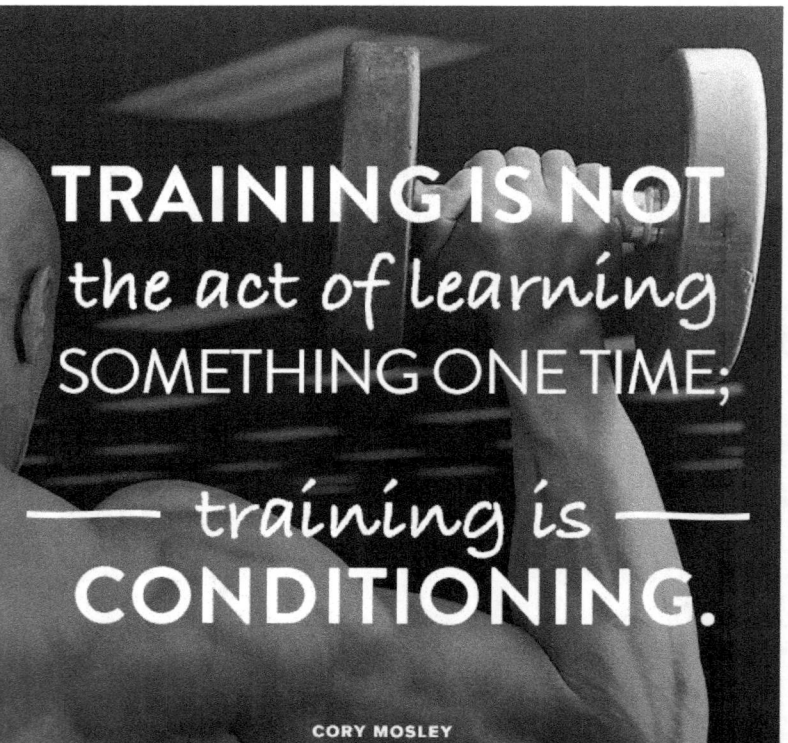

TRAINING IS NOT the act of learning SOMETHING ONE TIME; —— training is —— CONDITIONING.

CORY MOSLEY
FEARLESSWITHCORY.COM

Perseverance: The Key to Achieving Your Dreams

Succeeding on the first try every time sounds great, but the truth is that every good entrepreneur is going to have moments of great success followed by times of failure and discouragement. At times, it might feel like failure and discouragement come far more often than moments of success. If you are finding that failure and lack of progress have become a major part of your life, it is important to know that you are not alone.

Some of the most *successful people* in the world failed at first. For example, Walt Disney was fired from his job with a newspaper because he was said to lack creativity. Steven Spielberg was rejected three times by USC's film school. The first *Harry Potter* book was rejected multiple times. Yet in 2004, J. K. Rowling became the first billionaire author. The key to these people's success as well as the success of many other people is not that they found success right away, but that they continued to persist, not allowing their failures to stop them from achieving success. It is key to remember **perseverance breeds success.**[13]

REDEFINE FAILURE

When working toward achieving your goals, one of the top things you should do is refine failure. According to *Sara Blakely*, founder, owner, and CEO of Spanx growing up, her father would ask them what they had failed at that week. He would celebrate their failures with them. After a while, Blakely realized that failure was not about the end result as much as it was about not trying. Even as you face obstacles in your way, it is important to not give up or avoid doing something for fear of failure. Realize that real failure is quitting or not trying something. It is not about the obstacles that might be in your way along your path to success.[14]

CONTINUE TO PURSUE POSSIBILITIES

An *Entrepreneur* article from earlier this year talked about how Sivan Sternbach's art is hanging in the windows of Bergdorf Goodman in New York City. That wouldn't have happened, though, if Sternbach had not been persistent in working to achieve her dream. When she first emailed Bergdorf's senior director for visual presentation, she got a response within 48 hours. Yet, the director felt working with Sternbach would be too hard since she was based in Israel and not in the United States.[15]

Sternbach continued to email the senior director, even as she did not get a response. Finally, Sternbach realized she needed to send the director a sample of her work. She felt if he could see and touch her work, he would realize that his company needed it. Sternbach's persistence paid off. The important thing is to not get discouraged. If you know a specific path is right for you, don't let other people convince you otherwise. Continue to pursue the path until you have proved to others that you were right.

STAY FOCUSED

One of the biggest keys to persistence is staying focused. In life, it is easy to get distracted by other things. Sometimes, that means getting distracted by other people's negativity. It might mean getting distracted by less important tasks. You may even find yourself getting distracted by fear. If you want to follow through and achieve your dream, it is important to not allow yourself to be pulled away by distraction that will take your focus away from your dreams.

As you get distracted or discouraged, realize that if you quit before you achieve your dream, you are likely providing a path for someone else to **achieve the dream** you were too scared or unmotivated to achieve.[16] When you get discouraged, ask yourself if you can live with the "what ifs" associated with quitting. Then continue in pursuing your goal.

As you work to achieve your dreams, one of the most important things to realize is that there is no such thing as perfection. No matter how good you are at something, you will not succeed every time. For example, **Usain Bolt** had a 45-race winning streak at the Olympics and World Championships finals prior to the World Championships last August, where he came in third. No one is going to succeed at everything they attempt to do, but persistence is the key to finding those moments of success.[17]

SUCCESS
FINDS PEOPLE
Who
TAKE ACTION.

CORY MOSLEY
FEARLESSWITHCORY.COM

The Gift of Grit in Life and Business

Grit is defined as courage and resolve; strength of character, bravery, pluck, mettle, backbone, tenacity, steel, nerve, toughness, resolve, resolution, determination, tenacity, perseverance or endurance. In more colloquial terms, It's "big boy (or girl) undies on time" and "Winners never quit and quitters never win."

At no time in your life will grit get a bigger starring role than the day you realize the first step of entrepreneurship and open your own business. **Grit in life and business is key**. While other personality aspects and traits, such as vision, focus, and passion play important roles, your true test of entrepreneurial spirit reflects in your grit level through life and the business process.

WHY GRIT DETERMINES BUSINESS SUCCESS

- **Entrepreneurship is not a nine-to-five job,** it's an endless opportunity: Literally, in terms of hours and possible income and growth. There is no defined beginning, middle or end when it comes to your own business. It may start as a side gig, get sidelined when your regular job gets busy, pick up again seasonally and become your full-time employment as your client list grows. Unlike your "normal" job, working for yourself means working around your personal preferences and going when and where others need you.

- **Many people, including loved ones,** won't like you anymore: That reaction is often rooted in jealousy, distrust, their own laziness or misunderstanding your objectives. It's a courageous act to defy family and explain this dream as your new reality. They can love and support you or not, but you've made this decision.

- **Going your own way is a lonesome road:** You leave structure, friends, coworkers and everything you know about a "regular" life behind when you become an entrepreneur. Putting on the blinders and blocking out the daily noise requires a daily dose of backbone.

- **It's also expensive:** Plan a strategy to make and stick to a structured budget. Resolve to live within your means until your business takes off, and put your profits back into growing your business and paying off debt.

- **Failure tempts your return to the old way of doing things:** Grit provides the strength to stay the chosen course. Many entrepreneurs, including Stephen Spielberg, Walt Disney, Thomas Edison, Bill Gates and Madonna failed multiple times before catching that one successful idea.

- **Taking chances takes nerve:** Starting your own business is the classic flying leap with eyes closed; you can plan for a landing, but the exact location and your condition are uncertain. Starting with small jumps before the big leap builds grit.

HOW TO MAINTAIN YOUR GRIT FROM THE GET-GO

Live life balanced: Your own business is a lot of work, but it's important that it's not all work. Exercise, eat well, maintain personal friendships and find quiet time during those hectic days.

Find kindred spirits in your career quest: Join the chamber of commerce, local business club, Toastmasters or other organizations to help further your development. Check your local *MeetUp* website for groups and your business' national organization to see if there is a local chapter.[18]

Control what you can and flex with the rest: Flexibility is not a sign of weakness; it's a sign of understanding that not all situations are within your control. Exercise control where you can and give yourself options where control is impossible. Entrepreneurs handle unpleasant or unexpected business situations every day; how they deal with them provides great insight into the nature of the business owner.

Seek a professional mentor: Read their books, watch their videos and go to their live presentations. Many started young and now work with multinational corporations. That's not an overnight leap; that's years of grit and hard work to build that network.

Every Day presents an Opportunity to Take Action!

CORY MOSLEY
FEARLESSWITHCORY.COM

7 Ways to Stay Energized While Starting Your Own Business

Starting your own business is a great goal to pursue. However, if you're currently working a full-time job, you might find that keeping your energy levels high enough to work on your business is a chore. When your energy levels dip, your work starts to suffer, both for your current job and on your business. To try to prevent this, there are a few ways you can stay **energized** while starting your own business.

REGULAR EXERCISE

It might seem counter-intuitive, but forcing yourself to exercise regularly is important to keep your energy levels up. Exercise has been shown to increase the amount of energy we have throughout the day and helps to keep your mind clear and focused. No matter how busy you get, set aside some time each day — or every other day — to get in at least a quick workout.

A HEALTHY DIET

Along with exercise, you also need to have a healthy diet. Food is where our bodies get energy from, and so it's important that you are eating the right foods. Having too much sugar or carbs will slow you down, and make you feel sluggish. If you find that you are getting tired throughout the day, your diet is the first thing to examine.

GET ENOUGH SLEEP AT NIGHT

Another reason you might feel tired throughout the day is that you're not getting enough sleep. Too many people, when trying to start up their own business on the side, do so at the cost of a good night's rest. Make sure you are getting the recommended amount of sleep each night, no matter how much work you have to do.

STAY ORGANIZED

With so little time to work on your business, it's important to make sure you are getting as much done as you can during the few hours you have. By doing so, you'll check more items off of your to-do list, and as the result of seeing yourself accomplish things, feel more energized.

PRIORITIZE YOUR TASKS

As a part of organizing yourself, you should prioritize the things you need to do. This goes for not only business-related tasks but for everything in your life. If your business is important to you, perhaps you have to cut back on some of the other things you are doing in your life. By making your business a priority, and scaling back other aspects of your life, you'll have more energy to focus on what's important.

FIND MOTIVATIONAL MEDIA

A trick that works for many people is to find some motivational media to give you a boost. Perhaps it's a song, a movie, or a motivational speech online. Sometimes we just need something to pick us up when we're tired, and luckily there are a wide variety of options out there ready to help keep you energized.

SET ASIDE TIME FOR FUN

Finally, it's important that you give yourself some time to have fun and relax. If you are constantly working — both at your job and on your business — you'll quickly burn yourself out. Every once in a while you need to have some fun, or just take some time to relax. So schedule a night out with friends, or go get a massage. Your business will be waiting for you when you get back, and you'll be more energized to work on it.

If you are starting your own business on the side, and you find that you lack energy, don't stress. You are certainly not the first person who has experienced this, and there are plenty of ways to remedy it. You just need to pay more attention to how you are taking care of your body and mind and getting your life organized. If you can do the things mentioned above, you should find that you not only have more energy to work on your business, but you are able to get more meaningful work done when you do.

- Part 3 -

MATTERS OF RELATIONSHIPS

THE QUALITY OF
your life
IS THE QUALITY OF
your relationships.

- TONY ROBBINS

 FEARLESSWITHCORY.COM

How to Deal With Unsupportive Friends While Pursuing Entrepreneurship

Deciding to pursue entrepreneurship is a big decision. When you break out on your own, you need supportive people around you: those who are enthusiastic about your decision, willing to accept that you might have as much free time for a while, and even willing to help take some of the extra tasks off of your plate so that you have time to focus on your new business. Unfortunately, not everyone is going to be that supportive. How are you supposed to deal with them?

STEP ONE: BE CONFIDENT IN YOUR CHOICE

You didn't decide to embark on your entrepreneurship journey without thinking it through. Chances are, you took the time to seriously consider the pros and cons, plan your journey, and make sure that you were financially prepared for the sacrifices ahead. Now that you're ready, you don't have to answer to **unsupportive friends** who don't believe that you'll be able to accomplish what you've set out to do. Be confident in your choice and realize that you don't need other people to agree with you, especially when you've already talked it out with trusted mentors and those closest to you. Keep your head high and keep your confidence. You know you've got this!

STEP TWO: CHOOSE TO SKIP THE ARGUMENTS

Not everyone is going to understand the decisions that you make — and the truth is, even if you don't appreciate it, everyone is going to have an opinion. That doesn't mean, however, that you have to argue with the people closest to you as you embark on your journey. Instead, simply state, "You're welcome to your opinion, but I'm content with my decision." Then, move on. When you *don't engage*, the argument often loses its enjoyment.[19]

STEP THREE: SORT OUT THE DIFFERENCE BETWEEN AUTHENTIC FRIENDS AND OTHERS

You've acknowledged that your friends are welcome to their opinions, but you may still struggle with people who are simply unwilling to get behind you during this stage of your life — or even to keep their mouths shut when you need them to. On this journey, you'll learn a lot about who your friends are. When you encounter those relationships that simply aren't as strong as you thought they were, it's all right to decrease the amount of contact you have with them, especially during this part of your journey. Weed through the so-called friends who aren't really supportive of you and give yourself permission to spend less time with them or even end the relationship. You'll be amazed by how much lighter you feel.

STEP FOUR: SUCCEED!

There's nothing that silences naysayers quite as effectively as *getting results*. Plenty of people will tell you that you can't accomplish your goals or that you won't be able to succeed as an entrepreneur. Some of them can be silenced with a simple request. Others, however, will need to see those results before they realize that yes, you can accomplish everything that you set out to do.[20] When you come back as a successful entrepreneur with a growing business, the ability to set your own schedule, and the answer to all of your dreams, there's only so much they can say.

Dealing with unsupportive friends is a serious challenge for many entrepreneurs. Thankfully, you're not alone on your journey. You're surrounded by a community of people who believe in you and will support you as you work to reach your dreams — and you don't have to listen to the people who don't. Learning how to deal with those unsupportive individuals will help free you, giving you more time and energy to put into growing your business and seeing exactly what you can accomplish.

"IT IS NOT EASY
to FIND
HAPPINESS
in OURSELVES, *and*
IT IS NOT POSSIBLE
to FIND *it* ELSEWHERE."

– AGNES REPPLIER

 FEARLESSWITHCORY.COM

5 Reactions to Prepare For When You Share Your Dream of Entrepreneurship

The prospect of becoming an entrepreneur is exciting and motivating to budding business professionals. As you plan to **share your dream of entrepreneurship** with family and friends, you need to be prepared to receive a wide variety of responses. This is especially the case if you are the only person in your family who has considered becoming an entrepreneur. Below are five common reactions to entrepreneurship that you can expect to receive from family members when you share your entrepreneurship dream with them.

1. SHOCK.

Only *14 % of Americans are entrepreneurs.* The other 86% of Americans often do not understand why a loved one would want to leave the security of a good job to strike out on their own.[21] Family members who are shocked when you share your dreams might respond with a surprised expression and may say very little after you announce your news. Do not despair if you receive this reaction. Instead, you may wish to share some of the specific reasons that you decided to become an entrepreneur.

2. WORRY.

When some people think of entrepreneurship, they immediately begin to think of the negative aspects of starting a business. This can be disconcerting and upsetting to budding entrepreneurs seeking the support of their loved ones. Instead of focusing on the many positive aspects of starting a business, worriers are concerned that their loved ones may experience one or more of the following:

- A loss of stable income
- Regular exposure to business risks
- Stress generated by long work hours
- Sleepless nights and little time for recreation
- A lack of health insurance or benefits
- Overwhelming financial responsibilities

3. ENCOURAGEMENT.

In most cases, people who pursue entrepreneurship will have at least one family member who will immediately vocalize support and encouragement. Sometimes this support may arrive in the form of financial backing while other forms of support may include guidance and suggestions. Supportive family members are often a breath of fresh air to individuals who are considering entrepreneurship.

4. EXCITEMENT.

Many family members will react enthusiastically when you share your dreams about entrepreneurship with them. They will sense your own enthusiasm and respond in a way that mirrors your behaviors and emotions. Moreover, family members may respond with excitement due to one of the following reasons:

- They think you will become an overnight success
- They are delighted that you will now be your own boss
- They (often mistakenly!) think you will have more time to spend with them
- They believe you will immediately begin earning lots of money
- They envision a future of fame and fortune for you

5. ENVY.

Unfortunately, not all family members will respond with enthusiasm or genuine concern when you share your dreams. Many people who have thought about starting their own business choose not to pursue entrepreneurship because they lack the courage or drive to take the plunge. These individuals sometimes regret their decision to abandon their own entrepreneurial dreams and may be envious of friends or family members who have the courage to strike out on their own to pursue their dreams. Reactions tinged with envy are typically counterproductive and can derail your pursuit of your dreams if you give them too much weight.

THE BOTTOM LINE

Pursuing your entrepreneurship dream requires courage, motivation, and strategic planning. Sometimes sharing your dreams with your loved ones requires just as much courage as the pursuit of entrepreneurship. Ideally, your family members will ultimately provide support and guidance as you move forward on the path to starting your own business. Initially, however, you need to be prepared for a variety of reactions as you share your dreams with your loved ones. By understanding the five common reactions above, you can prepare yourself to handle your family's response when you share your dreams.

– Part 4 –
MATTERS OF BUSINESS

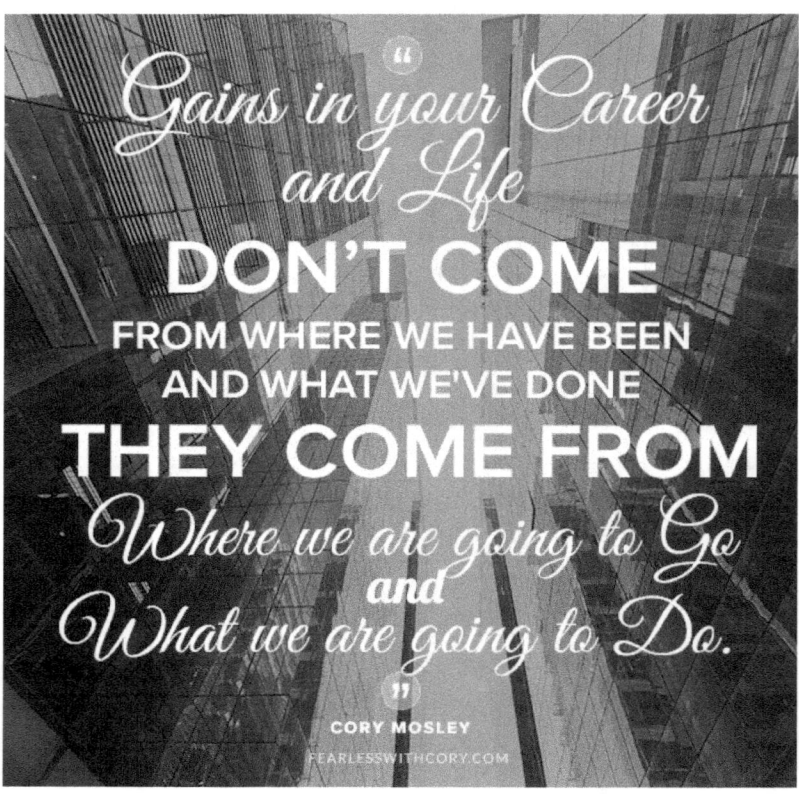

Gains in your Career and Life **DON'T COME** FROM WHERE WE HAVE BEEN AND WHAT WE'VE DONE **THEY COME FROM** *Where we are going to Go and What we are going to Do.*

CORY MOSLEY

FEARLESSWITHCORY.COM

The Power of Patience in Your Business

In today's world, it seems as though everything happens fast. You're encouraged to run at 100 miles per hour, never even slowing down to take a look around you.

> *When you're building your new business, however, patience is a valuable tool that can help you reach your goals and accomplish more than you ever dreamed.*

By employing patience in your everyday business interactions, you'll discover that you can take your business further than you dreamed.

WAIT FOR THE RIGHT OPPORTUNITIES

There's an opportunity on the horizon, and you're grasping after it with both hands — but is it the right opportunity for you? This is a key question that every business owner should ask before they move forward with their latest plans or opportunities. Instead of jumping in with both feet, take the time to carefully research and evaluate. If you're being urged to make an immediate decision, rather than taking the time you need to make a responsible decision for your business, then chances are this opportunity falls into the category of "too good to be true."

BUILD YOUR REPUTATION

There's something about patience that helps to *build the reputation* of many companies. When your contacts know that you're willing to wait, rather than diving in too fast or giving a gut response instead of a practical one, they'll improve their opinion of you and what you're able to accomplish within your business.[22] As a result, you'll have access to clients who might have, in the past, chosen to avoid your company simply because it was something new.

DEVELOP A BETTER CULTURE

You're not just trying to build your customer base. You're also trying to build your company into an amazing place where the top talent in your field is interested in working. When you **employ patience** as one of your key traits, you create an environment where people actually enjoy coming to work every day. Not only that, you're able to hold out for both talent and an individual who will fit more fully into your company culture, giving you an overall better employee base. You'll spend more time working with your *current employees* and less time shuffling employees or dealing with turnover — and that's an investment that can save your company both time and money in the long run.[23]

ACCEPT THE CHALLENGES AHEAD

Building a business means being surrounded by challenges. You'll often find yourself facing things that you didn't expect. With patience, you'll find yourself more than equal to those challenges, willing to dive in and face whatever is ahead for both you and your business. This commitment to sticking it out for the long haul, even if it means taking a longer road than you'd planned, can help you meet your goals and experience better success for the company as a whole.

BECOME A THOUGHT LEADER IN YOUR INDUSTRY

When you develop and use your patience on a regular basis, you'll find that it shows better wisdom as well as offering you better opportunities to *grow and learn.* You'll improve your personal skills and put yourself in a better position to accomplish things within your chosen industry — and that will help position you as a thought leader who is highly sought after by those looking for the best and brightest in your industry.

It's easy to run forward with both hands open, desperately grasping after any opportunity that comes your way. Harder is the long, slow road of patience — but in the end, patience will help build your business further and give you a better foundation. Ultimately, patience can be the difference between the success and failure of your business. Exercising that patience will help you reach your goals, even if it's a slower road than you'd planned.

IF YOU
DON'T BET
YOU DON'T
HAVE A
CHANCE TO WIN.

- FRANCIS FORD COPPOLA

FEARLESSWITHCORY.COM

Funding Your Startup With These Five Strategies

Now is a good time to be your own boss: more entrepreneurial job seekers *started their own business* by the end of 2016 than any year since 2009; especially heartening is the fact that over 85% of these startups were headed by someone age 40 and older. While many startup owners arrived there as the result of layoffs from high-tech companies, they are staying there because they understand the high-risk, high-stakes world of small business owners and both anticipate and accept the stresses and challenges.[24]

All startup businesses require some combination of talent, time, connections and capital. Of these four, capital is the most concrete need, yet sometimes the most difficult to find and the one you can easily abuse beyond your means. Before you sign that lease or hire that first employee, here are five ways to find **startup money** to fund your new venture:

YOUR OWN MONEY AND/OR MONEY FROM FRIENDS AND FAMILY

Private money from your savings, cashing out insurance policies and raiding your investment accounts is risky, because you're using the money you may need for retirement or to pay your basic living expenses. The upside of using your own money is that the only risk you take is with your own cash. If you fail, no one else gets hurt and you don't owe anyone a penny. You can also borrow or accept donations through a private fundraising effort or announce a crowdfunding campaign online. The people closest to you want to support your efforts and play a part in your success, and their financial contribution provides them with the means to brag later on about how they knew you when you were just starting out, but they knew you would make it big.

SMALL BUSINESS ADMINISTRATION LOANS AND GRANTS

The SBA helps you find and apply for federal and state grants available to your new business if it is set up as a nonprofit; you do not repay these funds. For-profit business startups can apply for *SBA*-assisted loans; you are matched with a lender-partner suited to your new venture's financial needs and arrangements are facilitated with the SBA.[25]

ANGEL INVESTORS

These individual investors are always looking for the next new idea in which to invest money, and their reward is a share of equity in your company. All transactions with an angel investor must be registered with the Securities and Exchange Commission; these are not back-alley deals. And if the idea of an angel to the rescue sounds a little fly-by-night, consider that companies such as Google and Yahoo were funded by angel investors, and these risk takers have their own groups, including *Band of Angels*[26], *AngelList*[27] and the *Angel Investment Network*[28], where they list and share information about new startups and opportunities.

VENTURE CAPITALISTS

These investors are similar to angel investors in that they have money to put into the next big idea, and expect equity shares in exchange for those funds. But unlike angels, venture capitalists also expect a voice in how your company operates. Both venture capitalists and angel investors want to make money as a result of their investment in your startup, but the angel investor is the equivalent of a silent partner, while the venture capitalist is akin to a member of your board of directors.

NONTRADITIONAL/ALTERNATIVE LENDING SOURCES

Banks, credit unions, family, and friends are the most traditional routes for raising money; online fundraising was considered nontraditional when it started, but with *$34 billion* raised by crowdfunding sources as of 2015, this method is no longer considered unusual. Alternative lending sources, such as *Paypal*[29], *On Deck*[30] and *Prosper*[31] are outside the banking industry's regulations but can provide startup capital with an online application completed in just a few minutes. Their interest rates, repayment schedules, fees and penalties are their own, and an entrepreneur who agrees to borrow from these sources must understand the difference in their terms and conditions versus a typical lending institution.

I've been in the business of building businesses since the age of 14, and I understand the thrill and the challenge of quitting life in corporate's world and creating your own. I've been successful at growing my businesses and helping others increase their profits and improve their operations because I've focused their ability to dig deeper for dedication, commit to a winning strategy and measure performance accurately.

DEFINE
YOUR SERVICE to others,
What you want to
ACCOMPLISH,
How you will **GET IT DONE,**
and **STATE THE OUTCOME**
as though it has
already taken place.

CORY MOSLEY
FEARLESSWITHCORY.COM

When You Start Your Business, Patience is Your Power Source

Sometimes, an idea for a new business will sit for years in your file drawer, computer docs or inside your head, just stewing, simmering but not gaining much momentum. Then one day, the one thing you've needed to go from dreams on paper to office-and-shingle reality shows up. Maybe it's the partner with deep pockets, a chance to team up with another like-minded entrepreneur and share space or the discovery of a new, better way to do what you love, make what you want and accomplish it faster, better, cheaper.

All of a sudden — you are moving faster than you thought possible and hiring staff and ordering office furniture and printing marketing materials and scheduling meetings and renting manufacturing space and the local press is calling for interviews and you're moving and it's too good to be true and —

Whoa. What just happened here? There's no time to think or breathe, no time for patience at a pace like that. Your new venture is outwardly fueled by passion, drive, and vision, but its main power source by patience. Here are five reasons why **exercising patience** before practice pays off:

YOUR NEW BUSINESS IS ALL ABOUT YOU—FOR NOW

Maybe at the start, it's just you and your hopes on a legal pad. Eventually, you'll have staff, human resources, a supply chain, clients, stockholders, and investors and you'll be responsible to their expectations. Exercising patience at the beginning of your venture means understanding the human nature of your business, not just the numbers, nuts and bolts. It paves the way for smart hiring, sound investing, happy clients and investors who cannot wait to be part of your company.

NOT EVERYONE SEES "THE LIGHT" AS FAST AS YOU DO

What's simply brilliant to you isn't simple or brilliant to everyone, at least not right away. A concept or product that makes a potential client happy, wealthy or simplifies their life in some way seems like an easy sell, but sometimes the most obvious ideas are the hardest to sell, which is frustrating to many new entrepreneurs, eager to immediately grow their business and make money. Exercising patience means education and enlightenment first, and the sales will follow.

BUILDING YOUR BRAND ISN'T AN OVERNIGHT OPTION

You build a following for your brand in a variety of ways;

digital marketing, meeting people at conventions, dinners, schools, and educational events and providing a website that reaches out to people, instead of waiting for them to find you. But brand building means finding innovative ways to stand out, such as partnering with a local nonprofit and linking to each other's websites, as well as working actively as a leader with the nonprofit. Staying active on social media with photos of yourself and your business doing positive things is not in keeping with the classic "sell, sell, sell!" mantra, but it patiently builds trust that builds a following that leads to business for your company.

LISTEN FIRST, COMPROMISE SECOND, ACT LAST

Patience is like using a feather duster when you'd rather use a battering ram to achieve your goals. You want to beat down competitors when you should study them, learn their best ideas and improve on them. You want to knock down clients' doors to grab deals, instead of understanding that while not all negotiations conclude successfully in a deal, all negotiations succeed if you learn something from those that fail for use the next time. Exercising patience means you whispered the door open, delicately disarmed the objections, concluded the discussion with compassion and came away better because you focused on listening, responding and then reached a decision.

TAKE TIME TO LEARN FROM THE EXPERT

I've helped business owners formulate strategies for growth and sales, and I know that takes time. I started my career as an entrepreneur at the age of 14, and while I believe there is no such thing as a goal that cannot be reached, I understand the power and practice of patience when it comes to assembling a strong sales team, increasing profits, improving processes and communications.

"

CREATE SEPARATION!

WHEN ALL THINGS ARE EQUAL,

you have a

50/50

chance to

WIN OR LOSE

WITH EACH PROSPECT.

"

CORY MOSLEY

FEARLESSWITHCORY.COM

5 Marketing Strategies for New Entrepreneurs

The word "marketing" brings up a mixed bag of responses. Some people love it. Others grimace and try to change the topic. Some recognize marketing as a necessity to successful entrepreneurship. Others balk at the idea of sounding salesy, spending money, or being inauthentic.

Regardless of your feelings, marketing is essential for entrepreneurs. It's the only way to effectively share your message and draw in leads (who then become clients). Luckily, it doesn't need to be overwhelming, inauthentic, or even expensive. By keeping these five marketing strategies in mind, you can enter any campaign with confidence:

1. KNOW YOUR AUDIENCE

The most important action you can take before beginning your **marketing efforts** is learning as much as possible about your audience. Until you know who you're marketing to, you won't know how to market to them. This means starting conversations, paying attention to language, and building relationships.

From a practical perspective, this step involves diving into both the demographic and psychographic information that makes up your audience. Are you serving mothers? Entrepreneurs? Technology start-ups? Is your audience comprised of women, men, or both? Are you focusing on young adults or retirees? All of these questions are important, and they only represent the tip of the iceberg.

In addition to knowing the basic makeup of your audience, it's also important to know their emotional state. What do they hope for? On the other hand, what do they fear? How do they spend money and why? What words do they use to describe their frustrations?

Begin building a file of information that pertains directly to your audience. This file will become indispensable during your marketing efforts.

2. DECIDE ON YOUR INVESTMENT

There are two ways to invest in your marketing efforts. On the one hand, there is a time investment. On the other, there's a monetary investment.

Most marketing campaigns consist of a combination of both time and money. It's up to you to evaluate your resources and decide which investment makes the most sense. If you decide that a time investment makes the most sense for your business then you will be more concerned with active relationship building and organic growth through social media, articles, interviews, and more.

If you choose to invest with money, you may be looking at running paid ads or hiring a sales strategist. Generally, a monetary investment will see faster results, but both can be highly effective.

3. CREATE A DETAILED ACTION PLAN

All too often, new entrepreneurs will approach marketing without intention. A solid marketing plan is based on audience research, a reasonable time frame, and data. Unfortunately, many marketing plans aren't approached with that much clarity.

Often, what happens is this:

> *An entrepreneur gets an idea for an offer. They get excited about the offer and start creating marketing content. They blast the content out to the world. Then they wait... And wait... And wait. What went wrong?*

Without a plan in place, there's no audience research to direct your marketing. Without a time frame and conversion goals, there's no way to measure success or know what to tweak. And without an eye on data, there's no real indication of how the marketing campaign is going.

When you're ready to begin marketing, set parameters around your efforts. Establish benchmarks and check in with your campaigns regularly.

4. BE FLEXIBLE

The beauty of the online world is that it is constantly changing. And if your marketing efforts are limited to online, they will also be changing. This presents a constant stream of new opportunities, while also turning into a bit of a headache.

The key here is flexibility. As entrepreneurs, we need to be willing to adjust and adapt with the times. As social media platforms, paid advertising, and search engine optimization evolve, so should we. Of course, we shouldn't be chasing after every shiny object that crosses our path. A new social media platform pops up every day. Does that mean we need an account on all of them? No. But it does mean we should pay attention to the trends, and adjust as needed.

5. PAY ATTENTION TO METRICS

This may be the most important factor when it comes to your marketing efforts, though it's the least exciting. Data-driven marketing campaigns are far more effective than those with no eye for metrics. When you know your conversion rates, lead acquisition, and response rates you can make better decisions overall.

Make it a habit to check in with your data frequently, but don't obsess over every individual lead. Instead, look at the big picture. All too often an entrepreneur will throw a marketing campaign out, presuming it failed. In reality, it simply didn't have enough reach to produce the desired numbers. Know the conversion rates for your industry, and make sure your marketing efforts are seen by enough people before you make a decision.

MARKETING IS A NON-NEGOTIABLE FOR ENTREPRENEURS

Whether you love marketing or hate it, it's a necessary piece of entrepreneurship. Your message is only going to reach your audience if you put it out to the world, and the more focused and streamlined your efforts, the faster they will pay off.

SEEK OUT **TRAINING** *that improves* YOUR **COMMUNICATION**

CORY MOSLEY
FEARLESSWITHCORY.COM

5 Essential Entrepreneurial Skills Entrepreneurs Invest Into Themselves

Being an entrepreneur requires more than having an innovative idea. A dream is what gets you started, but certain skills are needed to keep you going. Successful entrepreneurs invest in themselves. They develop the skills necessary to succeed even if they don't have them from the beginning. In fact, that may be the reason why it takes most startups years to gain traction and momentum. Usually, the product or the service is somewhat the same 7 years after the startup as it was when it first began.

So, what changed?

Often it is the skill set of the entrepreneur involved that changes. It grows to possess the skills that are essential to entrepreneurial success.

So, what are the skills entrepreneurs need to get ahead?

There are actually 5 essential entrepreneurial skills. Let's glance at each of them together.

1. RESOURCEFULNESS

One of the exciting things about entrepreneurship is that it is all up to you. You aren't dependent on a coworker doing their job. You don't have to worry about a boss letting you thrive or holding you back. The buck stops with you.

What entrepreneurs realize soon after starting, however, is that this increase in freedom comes with increased responsibility. Just as you don't have a boss telling you what to do, you likewise don't have one you can go to when things don't work out. You've got to figure it out yourself. When your team doesn't have the tools they need, you have to provide them. Whether you know what those tools are or not is irrelevant. You are responsible for the organization. Its success or failure is up to you. That is exciting. And it also requires an extreme amount of resourcefulness — an ability to get whatever job done that needs to get done when it needs to be done.

2. RESILIENCY

Entrepreneurship is tough. It is rife with setbacks and disappointments. You will feel misunderstood. Things won't work out the way you hoped. This is especially true in the beginning. It takes a lot of strength to push on in spite of facts that say what you're doing isn't going to work. Financial problems arise. Relationship tensions rub. Stress erupts.

Before you jump, you are full of excitement. After the leap, reality hits. And reality hurts. You've got to be resilient to bounce back from the falls, to keep going against adversity. And sometimes you will have to motivate other people to do the same when everything inside of you is yelling quit.

3. SALES

Selling is a skill. And regardless of the industry, you are in, you are in sales. You have to sell your ideas to get started, sell yourself to get a team and sell your product or service to get a profit.

This is true for every field. You may, for example, be a writer. You focus on writing. But have you ever heard of a best-writing author? Neither have I. But we've both heard of a best-selling author. Why? Because regardless of the field you're in, you are a seller. Entrepreneurs with this skill are ahead of others who don't.

4. DISCIPLINE

Discipline is doing what you don't want to do in order to achieve what you want to accomplish.

It's nice to feel like we are our own boss. But the implications of that is that you are both the boss and the employee. You have to be a strong enough boss to push yourself and hold yourself accountable regardless of how you feel. And at the same time, you have to be a good enough employee to listen to yourself and do what you are supposed to do. That sounds like heaven when you're stuck in a 9-5. But when it becomes your reality and you are the one who pays the consequences for a lack of discipline, it's an entirely different story.

It is also important to note that most entrepreneurs think they have self-discipline. Then they become entrepreneurs and realize they don't. It is a skill that can't truly be assessed when you have a boss holding you accountable Only after you launch on your own will you find out if you have this skill or not. And if you don't, you will have to develop it or get out of entrepreneurship. It is, unfortunately, that simple.

5. EFFICIENCY

At first glance, you may think being disciplined and being efficient are the same thing.

Not quite.

You cannot be efficient unless you're disciplined. But just because you have self-discipline doesn't mean you know how to work efficiently. Discipline is simply about doing it. Making it happen. Efficiency is about making sure that the thing you're doing is what you're supposed to be doing at that time and then doing it as quickly as you can without compromising the integrity of excellence. Discipline is not wasting time. Efficiency is about making the most optimal use of the time you use. Here is where you prioritize. You do the 20% of tasks that give you 80% results. You work in your lane. You delegate. Discipline is necessary for an entrepreneur to even start seeing a profit. Efficiency is what is required to take the organization to the next level.

This list could be extended as other skills are important.

But important and essential aren't the same. It's safe to say that a deficit in even one of these five skills will have devastating effects on an entrepreneur's success. Many times, the entrepreneur who feels stuck isn't in a rut because of a flawed service or defective product. It is usually a lack of one or more of these five essential entrepreneurial skills.

Unfortunately, many entrepreneurs fight blindly on fixing teams, systems, strategies, etc. But they do not spend the time focusing on these skills. In those cases, the skills develop naturally over time. Usually. This is because the nature of entrepreneurship forces one to may these changes simply to survive. But entrepreneurs who are aware that the leak in the ship is not what they sell but is in fact in their own set of skills, the focus can shift to developing the lacking skills. And when that happens, major breakthroughs follow.

"I BELIEVE
MOST PEOPLE
FAIL IN LIFE
SIMPLY BECAUSE THEY
MAJOR IN
MINOR THINGS."

- TONY ROBBINS

5 Productivity Techniques for Entrepreneurs Looking to Optimize

Being an entrepreneur is all about getting as much done as humanly possible, especially if you're still a "One Man Band" trying to do everything by yourself before the business is ready to support employees. For the eager and ambitious, you know that the key to achieving more is to do more, but where do you find the time? Assuming 8 hours for sleep, there are 16 hours in a day to run your business, balance your finances, provide customer service, run errands, maintain your relationships and finish your household chores before another necessary sleep cycle. Instead of stressing out about what you miss or letting your personal life slip in favor of other demands, here are 5 great tips for becoming a smoother, more time **efficient** you.

1: GET ENERGIZED

You are not the sitcom character who wakes up grumpy,

needs coffee, and hates going to work. You are an energetic, motivated entrepreneur eager to achieve bigger and better goals every day. From the moment your feet hit the floor, remember that you are a supreme badass who can handle everything life dishes up. This positive attitude will give you the right forward momentum to take on your daily goals and enjoy crossing each item off your agenda as you achieve it. The coffee helps, of course, but you don't need it to love your job and enjoy your day.

2: PLAN LIKE WITH LIKE

You can maximize efficiency by planning to take care of similar tasks together rather than losing time on two separate trips or efforts. If, for instance, you need to pick up groceries and stop by the bank, plan to do them together and pick venue locations that are near each other to save time needlessly driving across town. Everything can be done more efficiently from making a week's worth of healthy lunches on Monday to writing emails while you wait for an important phone call because you're already stopped for a moment at your desk. Using a practical grouping approach with everything will save little slices of time throughout your schedule.

3: SET ALERTS

Don't be afraid to use technology to help you out. There are many disorganized entrepreneurs but your business can be perfectly tidy with the assistance of scheduling software and automatic alerts. The selection of applications on your smartphone alone are more than enough to keep a determined person organized. However, if you've struggled with complex organizer apps with little improvement in your personal efficiency, the solution might be to go simpler instead. From post-it notes to email alerts, integrate your digital reminders in ways that work with your day and don't take too much time to manage.

4: TIME YOURSELF

You may not realize how much time you spend on each task. Instead of just trying to get faster and stressing out when you don't, motivate yourself and prove that you're speeding up by constantly timing your activities. Start with no-pressure baselines. Keep a stopwatch program open and practice starting and stopping it as you begin and end activities. You will start to get an idea of how long you typically take on timed tasks and then can work to beat your times and become probably faster. Soon, you'll be working comfortably in double-time and can earn yourself several minutes a day of time saved via simple efficiency.

5: KEEP SCORE

Nothing motivates like beating your own high score. If you really want to become more time efficient, keep a score as if efficiency were a game. Assign points to complete work tasks, errands, chores, and even personal hobbies. Give yourself a bonus point for every activity you did faster than the day before and try to beat your daily or weekly scores. Just remember to be a fair score-keeper for yourself or results will inevitably skew.

The key to super-efficient time management is a constant energetic effort. If you want to be a more efficient business owner and constantly challenge yourself to do so, you will get faster. Time management is all about saving every second. By moving quickly, not daydreaming, and getting a little faster each day you will quickly find yourself achieving 7 or more impossible things before breakfast.

– Part 5 –

THE HOW I MAKE MONEY (H.I.M.M.) FRAMEWORK

One of the most common areas of frustration for me when working with entrepreneurs is when I can't get answers to questions like how much does your product or service cost? What's your margin? What are your financial needs and goals?

So I decided to create a resource to help aspiring entrepreneurs and even those that had started a business already achieve some clarity and data around their business which I named the H.I.M.M. Framework or How I Make Money.

The framework consists of 14 steps that will help you identify and answer some key questions about your business, your needs, and the potential for both to thrive instead struggle.

Let's get to work.

HOW I MAKE MONEY

WITH CORY MOSLEY

01 Who is my customer/buyer?

02 What products/services do I provide?

03 What are my operating costs?

04 How much is my product or service?

HOW I MAKE M$NEY

WITH CORY MOSLEY

05 What is my profit margin?

06 What are my revenue needs?

07 What are my revenue goals?

08 How much of my product or service do I need to sell to meet my financial goals?

HOW I MAKE MONEY

WITH CORY MOSLEY

09 How much of my product or service do I need to sell to meet my financial needs?

10 How much can I invest in the business?

11 How will I acquire customers?

12 How long to achieve break even?

HOW I MAKE M$NEY

13 What training do I already have?

14 What training do I need to be successful?

NOTES

My Personal Mantra

KEEP THE MIND
SHARP
THE VISION
CLEAR
THE RESOLVE
STRONG
&YOU WILL
MAKE IT

CORY X MOSLEY

Acknowledgments

There are simply people who come along and impact you whether they know it or not, and those whom which things would just be different if they weren't around. I'd like to thank a few of those people at this time.

My wife Xiomara
Mom
The whole Mosley clan
Carlos & Simone
Sean & Karen
Paul & Christy
William
Kwame
Mike & Mary
Jamal & Liz
Michele
Brandon
Willie & Dee
Delatorro
Grant & Elena
El Patronn
Gary
Jason
Todd

Thank you!

End Notes

1. "Working in a gig economy", Bureau of Labor Statistics, May 2016, https://www.bls.gov/careeroutlook/2016/article/what-is-the-gig-economy.htm

2. "The Impostor Phenomenon", The Journal of Behavioral Science, October 2011, https://www.tci-thaijo.org/index.php/IJBS/article/view/521

3. "12 Leaders, Entrepreneurs and Celebrities Who Have Struggled With Imposter Syndrome", Entrepreneur, November 2017 https://www.entrepreneur.com/slideshow/304273

4. "7 Reasons People With Impostor Syndrome Struggle to Succeed", Inc, https://www.inc.com/amy-morin/7-reasons-people-with-impostor-syndrome-struggle-to-succeed.html?cid=search

5. "The Science of Laughter", Psychology Today, June 2016, https://www.psychologytoday.com/us/articles/200011/the-science-laughter

6. "One Neuroscientist Explains The Science of Laughter", wbur, December 2016, https://www.wbur.org/hereandnow/2016/12/13/science-of-laughter

7. The science of laughter, BBC News, September 2016, https://www.bbc.com/news/health-37311320

8. "Really Want to Make Someone's Holiday? Science Says You Should Give This Type of Gift", Inc., December 2016, https://www.inc.com/jessica-stillman/3-super-athletes-share-their-secrets-of-exceptional-mental-toughness.html?cid=search

9. "Forget Big-Picture: Why You Should Build Mental Toughness Through Small Steps", Inc. Video, https://www.inc.com/video/amelia-boone/why-build-mental-toughness-through-small-steps.html

10. "What Climbing Mount Kilimanjaro Taught Me About Climbing 'Mount Entrepreneur', Entrepreneur, June 2017, https://www.entrepreneur.com/article/296182

11. Mind Games, https://www.mindgames.com/

12. "Regular exercise releases brain chemicals key for memory, concentration, and mental sharpness", Harvard Men's Health Watch, May 2013, https://www.health.harvard.edu/press_releases/regular-exercise-releases-brain-chemicals-key-for-memory-concentration-and-mental-sharpness

13. "29 famous people who failed before they succeeded", Business Insider, July 2015, https://www.businessinsider.com/successful-people-who-failed-at-first-2015-7/#rah-winfrey-was-publicly-fired-from-her-first-television-job-as-an-anchor-in-baltimore-for-getting-too-emotionally-invested-in-her-stories-2

14. "Learning to celebrate failure at a young age led to this billionaire's success", Business Insider, May 2017, https://www.businessinsider.com/sara-blakely-spanx-ceo-offers-advice-redefine-failure-retail-2017-5

15. "The Secrets to Reaching Your Goals Are Persistence, Confidence and a Belief in Yourself", Entrepreneurs, August 2017, https://www.entrepreneur.com/article/299453

16. "5 Ways to Master the Persistence That Makes a Great Entrepreneur", Entrepreneur, July 2017, https://www.entrepreneur.com/article/297040

17. "7 Lessons on Failure You Can Learn From Top Athletes", Entrepreneur, October 2017, https://www.entrepreneur.com/article/300699

18. MeetUp, https://www.meetup.com/?_cookie-check=teFQq7OJPA4qJ1A6

19. "How to Deal With Unsupportive Friends and Family", Entrepreneur, January 2014, https://www.entrepreneur.com/article/230721

20. "How to Deal With Unsupportive Family and Friends", HuffPost, December 2016, https://www.huffpost.com/entry/how-do-deal-with-unsuppor_b_8856004

21. "The U.S. Now Has 27 Million Entrepreneurs", Inc., September 2015, https://www.inc.com/leigh-buchanan/us-entrepreneurship-reaches-record-highs.html

22. "8 Ways Practicing Patience Radically Increases Your Capacity for Success", Entrepreneur, September 2015, https://www.entrepreneur.com/article/250211

23. "Importance of patience in the workplace", Career & Education, February 2013, https://careerandeducation. expertscolumn.com/importance-patience-workplace

24. "Why It's a Good Time to Start Your Own Company", Fortune, February 2017, https://fortune.com/2017/02/22/ startups-2017-challenger/

25. SBA, https://www.sba.gov/

26. Band of Angels, https://www.bandangels.com/

27. AngelList, https://angel.co/

28. Angel Investment Network, https://www. angelinvestmentnetwork.us/angel-investor-groups

29. PayPal, https://www.paypal.com/webapps/ workingcapital/

30. OnDeck, https://lendedu.com/blog/ondeck-business-loans/

31. Prosper, https://www.prosper.com/

About the Author

Cory Mosley, CSP is an award-winning Business Growth Catalyst, Professional Speaker, and Coach that helps entrepreneurs and business owners tackle and overcome their most pressing challenges so their business can grow.

A life-long entrepreneur since the age of 14, Cory made a name for himself in the Automotive Industry where his consulting and training company clients included global organizations like VW North America, Mercedes-Benz, Volvo USA, BBDO, Berkshire Hathaway and Urban Science.

Today he is a sought-after expert on business growth strategies and keynotes events, consults with businesses, and coaches' entrepreneurs that are truly committed to achieving their goals.

As a media personality Cory has hosted programs on The Atlanta Small Business Network, i-Heart Radio, and currently hosts his widely distributed Fearless Entrepreneurship Podcast where he interviews everyday entrepreneurs working to build great businesses.

When not working with clients or speaking at events Cory can be found at home in Richmond, Virginia with his wife and two Brussel Griffons Zack and Rozy Bear.

For More Information:

Cory would love to connect with you, please connect with him on any and all of the following Social Networks.

Facebook: /fearlesswithcory
Instagram: /officialcorymosley
Twitter: /corymosley
YouTube: /corymosley

Listen to the Fearless *Entrepreneurship* Podcast across the following Networks.

Apple Podcast
Spotify
Google Play
Sticher Radio
IHeartRadio
Radio Republic

To learn more about Cory's programs go to CoryMosley.com.

If you would like to hire Cory to speak at your event please contact xiomara@corymosley.com or call +1 804-384-0447.

Finally, if you received value from this book please share it with us by emailing connect@corymosley.com